CROSSING OVER
TO
THE SECRET WITNESS

FRANK ROMANO

Published by AB Film Publishing
290 W. 12th Street, Suite A
New York, NY 10014

To my Mother (Always with me, my soul) and my Kids (My life)

&

To passion, to my spiritual brothers and sisters, and most of all, to the
Pure Light Love Spirit,
our ultimate guide.

TABLE OF CONTENTS

ACKNOWLEDGEMENTS

Special thanks go to Lorna Romano who carefully edited my new poems (*Recent Poems: 2009-2018*) integrated into this book. Her meticulous mind and mastery of the English language greatly enhanced the possibility of conveying the messages imbedded in my poems. Ruth Wire, writer and playwright carefully edited the original poems (Poems: 1970-2008) gestating since high school. She has an uncanny feel for even the most obscure images projected by my prose, often written during trance-like meditations, without changes, and derived from my total "me".

I thank Tom Romano, my brother, the exceptional artist who designed the cover as well as illustrated some of the poems. His great artistic patience overcame my instructions which were almost as mystical as some of my poems.

I want to also thank my English teacher at Santa Rosa High School, Mr. Hansen, who inspired me to let my heart speak....

Finally, this book is dedicated to pure passionate unconditional love from the heart and extending to all through the pure love spirit.

INTRODUCTION

"Impossible not to feel more alive after reading Frank Romano's volcanic bursts of poetry."

—Ruth Wire, Poet, HayWire Writers' Workshop

I have often longed to open my heart to the unconditional Love spirit. This work allows me to finally do that!!

My mother, who recently passed to the next world, was the first to open it and was always my model for loving and giving unconditionally. Years before she passed, I had already dreamed that I would join her and my daughter, Victoria, in the next world, upon their deaths.

Upon awakening, I wrote the dream down exactly as I remembered it. It is included in this book under the title, "Time Warp." Later, I interpreted its origin as deriving from recent experiences caregiving my mother in Ashland, Oregon, and co-parenting Victoria in Paris, France.

Years before caregiving my mother, I was with my daughter, Victoria, when she began suffocating, even turning blue, after choking on a peach peel. Fortunately, I was able to make her gag a bit by placing my finger gently down her throat, which dislodged the peel allowing her to breathe and to revive.

During the time I was caregiving mother, I was, along with other family members, able to help pull her from the shrouds of possible death in the hospital. Afterwards, I was a bit burned out and traumatized, while having strong emotions surrounding that experience, notably thinking that I would rather die than feel the pain of my mother's death. My mother later returned from the hospital, almost normal. I subsequently had several serious anxiety attacks, spent nights with her, drained, and later dreamed "Time Warp."

Caveat: My poems often express uncontrolled outbursts from my heart. As such, I don't recommend them to those who shy away from unmasked, unadulterated raw bone emotions.

Frank Romano, Paris, France, March 2nd, 2020

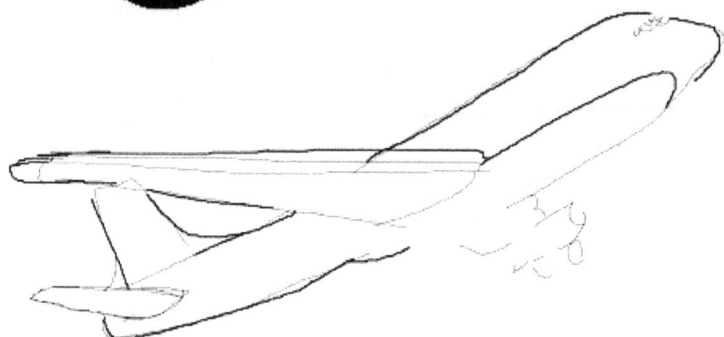

Secret Witness

I watched a movie
last night
in flight
And it slammed me— hard!
  I couldn't stop pouring out
  Tears streaming down
  So much
  Couldn't stop
  Nothing I could do . . .
And for once,
I let it go
I let it all go
and didn't push the memories away
as I've been doing for years.
I thought of you-
I thought of our joy-
Reuniting in Paris-
The birth of our children-
Your sorrowful eyes as you looked across-
the snow-covered courtyard, from our hovel
  in the Paris public housing . . . the projects-
Of your giving birth to a dead foetus
  Pushing, with my encouraging cries,
  with such raw, desperate power
  that you defecated on the operating table
  But I cleaned it up with joy, with love
      Happy just to be there for you
      and you smiled
      I did it before the doctor could see the brown blob
      in the middle of the white sheets
      Before he had returned,
      after carrying our dead son away
      from our loving clutches
So many seconds, minutes, hours, days of pure joy

And then despair
The risks I've taken in the Holy Land for peace, for freedom
    were necessary,
    following a calling I had,
    long before I met you
But I embraced the danger
    even sometimes risked my life,
    to be faithful to my calling
    Even as the dim fog surrounding us and our unbridled,
    often insanely obsessive passion disappeared
    I desperately embraced my calling
    so fervently,
    especially following our midnight trysts
    and our sometimes-disrupted late night rendezvous
        in a North Beach café, at our Italian hideaway
        as voluptuous Italian *parole di amore* flowed from my lips to
yours.
            Red *vino di amore* chased by animal sounds, raw passion
                Violent ardor, unintelligible words, raw to the
            bone. . .
                Unfrocked, desperation clawing at my heart. . .to
            the bone. . .
                Spasms of uncontrolled motions
    We lapped up those moments rare but there
        to torment me, to *matar* me later
It may have made it a little easier, taking those steps into darkness
    in the Middle East,
    thinking I would never see your eyes
    glistening in the mist . . .
        Beams from San Francisco streetlights
        shining through the window
        The faint foghorns echoing
        as you lay there, cozy beside me
            steaming with the funky scents, after a night of sweaty
        embraces, our infant
            darlings warmly snoozing in bed near us
Let the tears be my witness, that all those years

have never tempered this irrational, uncontrollable urge
to hold you . . . again.
So, I finally figured it out this moment
    years after our final *adieu*
    as the plane engines droned on into the night
        over the deep, dark azure stretch,
   over the Atlantic
       from New York City to Paris
That from the very second of our last moment,
     when I saw your flaring rear taillights flashing away from me years
  before,
    from our early morning undulations serenaded by gulls
        soaring up and away, into the mist above Coit Tower
      as I stood there, frozen by the icy ocean winds buffeting my
      numbed face,
    I knew . . .
  It would be our last night and
       you'd be forever away from my arms
          even though I would still, for days—for years—be reaching
      out into the night,
        trying to pull you and your indifferent car back to me
I still sometimes woke up suffocating, choking, sweat dripping . .
It all finally came together—I figured out, some 40,000 feet above sea level
    why I had plunged into my work,
    travelling far, far away
to escape the wrenching pain, after all those years,

Because that night, in the windy streets of San Francisco,
    in spite of my loves—my kids, my mom and life yet to breathe—,
    in spite of my faith,
At that second, that very second
    when it ended, something deep inside. . . of me. . .died.

By Frank Romano, in a plane hovering over the Atlantic, between New
York City and Paris, January 24th, 2018

Backwoods

The day after an author event at a local bookstore, the author spent the morning with his hosts in a converted farmhouse in the back country, about an hour from Charlotte, N. Carolina. They recounted stories of the area, the people and the difficulties for African Americans that had lived there and those who had tried to move there. Later that day, while jogging in the beautiful forested back country, the author's scanning of the peaceful surroundings bathed in colorful fall foliage was interrupted by my his musings, in particular by FLASHES of yesteryear.

Drops of real mountain dew
dot my windowsill
as I put on my shoes before I head out jogging,
down the narrow country road.
Shimmering light from the cabin
        behind the black silhouette
        of the pick-up truck
Dogs nestled near the steps
   The mama sighs
        amid the jostling of the
        squealing puppies
        contentedly suckling
The wind shifts, filtering gently through the yellow-brown leaves
        Trees of yesteryear
The gurgling of the mountain stream, surfing
        sun-crisped leaves
Dogs bark and people shuffle down their driveways, children
   steer their three wheelers among scattered toys
   Good ole boys stirring in chairs on their rickety wooden porches
drinking beer, smoking, wave at me,
      their ruddy faces creased with the tread of rugged years on the
farm, checkered smiles flashing as they bat at bustling flies . . .

FLASH:

A hangman's noose
    A strained gurgling from the thrashing black man's throat
    the vision of daunting white hoods
    The last kicks ruffle the air, then stillness . . . silence . . .
    the rope creaks as the stiffening body slowly turns
    in the middle of the forest, alone

As I jogged, a picket fence, a lopsided sign, with letters missing:
    Com_ to _he Lord

FLASH:

Country breakfast, I am the guest
    Eggs collected from proud banty hens strutting in the front yard, delectably scrambled
    hot cakes bathed in local maple syrup
    The bearded father, skin reddened from the sun, smiles
    through crooked teeth
    kindly, nodding as he watches me eat, squinty-eyed smiles

I stop jogging and walk up the pathway leading to one of a myriad country churches, eye the steeple above
    A sense of warning stirs . . .

FLASH:

Back to the country home, where I am the guest again
    In front of the fire, he kneads the silky fur of a cocker spaniel
    nudging close to him
    The small head of a young child with golden curls lies resting on his lap,
    Emitting the song of deep, peaceful breathing . . .

I start up again, jogging to the grass on the right to let a pick-up truck rumble onwards. As it passes, the metal casings of two rifles—stacked one on top of the other—flash through the window, next to a flimsy broom waving and jolting with the truck's movement . . .

FLASH:

The loving father hovers over his child, shaking his head at the scene below him, smiling with paternal care
    Then the door cracks open and he slithers out into the blackness,
    a white robe curled over his muscular arm

Frank Romano, Manhattan, New York City, February 2015

Empty Seat

Empty seat where a Palestinian child should be
    but he was killed with live fire.

An Israeli soldier was to return from war

    but he didn't come back.

From an Israeli sniper?

    Shooting hot metal

at a young Palestinian boy with rock in hand,

    way beyond David & Goliath!

Played out daily with martyrs and tears falling

    into the hot sands of the West Bank and Gaza.

Empty seat ascending

upwards, upwards

toward the swirling sky and then descending

onto the platform,

but nobody enters

and "La grande roue" shimmers and stirs

 as the empty seat rises,

slightly swaying

in the wind.

Ramallah, November 2018

7

Hobo camp

The author woke up one night and wrote down the following dream, without making any major changes. It was about a small rural town, Los Molinos, California, where he used to live with his family. He was 10 years old, in the 5th grade. All 5th graders were bused to a school in an even smaller town, Tehama, because there were no classes for them in Los Molinos. On its way there, the bus would drive by a field and a creek, where hobos were encamped.

The school bus stops
on the corner
opens its doors
A child wearing a baseball cap
gets in
dragging his shiny lunch pail
up and over the steps

Out the window, I look
across the field
to the hobo camp
A trail of smoke winds
over the trees
Underneath a fire burns

The door closes and
the bus starts up again
My eyes follow the trees
    'til the smoke
        dissipates, like a memory . . .

Now, many moons later,
I look out across the meadow,
Not from the bus, but this time,
from the bank of the creek
My eyes follow the bus
stopping at the corner

Back in time, my bus returns
later that afternoon from school
taking me home to chickens
cackling in our garden
taking me back . . .
My rooster will be there,
waiting for my return

Years later, again, the bus stops,
the door opens;
the bus plods onward
as glow from my deep-set
aging eyes. . .

below
the only decoration
on a gaunt, stubbled face
sweep across the field

. . .to meet my youthful eyes
beaming from the bus
 an ethereal collision!

Stops again, 50 yards ahead,
The door opens, no one gets out,
no one enters
The bus starts up,
its motor whining . . .

Back in time again,
I'm at the house, alone
I walk the garden
It's quiet
No shouting kids
Dad's gone

No more chickens
No bros, no sis
Ma's voice fades away
into the breeze
Sifting through the fronds
of palm trees overhead.

But I'm still there
in front of the hearth
feeding the low, sputtering fire
in the empty house
The staircase strains, and squeaks—
footsteps from the past?
as I look out the front window . . .

To the future, again,
I lean over
From the rolled-up sleeve
of my patched overalls
my bony hand protrudes
feeding the fire with a twig,
in the meadow,
next to the creek,
A can half-buried in the coals,
gently simmering . . .

The rumble of the bus
I shift my gaze to see it there
on the corner,
waiting, waiting . . .

Frank Romano, Limeil-Brévannes, France 2009

Time Warp

The following was a dream. Upon awakening, the author wrote it down exactly as he remembered it. Later, he interpreted its origin as deriving from a recent experience caregiving his mother and years earlier when his daughter, Victoria, was suffocating, even turning blue, after choking on a peach peel. Fortunately, he was able to make her gag a bit, by placing his finger gently down her throat, which dislodged the peel allowing her to breathe and to revive.

During the time he was caregiving his mother, he was, along with other family members, able to help pull her from the shrouds of possible death in the hospital. Afterwards, he was a bit burned out and traumatized, while having strong emotions surrounding that experience, notably thinking that he would rather die than feel the pain of his mother's death. His mother later returned from the hospital, almost normal. He subsequently had several serious anxiety attacks, spent nights with her, drained, and then later dreamed this:

Sat by mom at home.
Her blue eyes on my worried brown ones,
she smiled, her courage stretching the dried lips.

Before she went to sleep, I put her arm around my head.

She tilted her head over to me and said, "Frankie, so glad you're here.
Don't leave me! Don't leave me!"
"Mom, I won't leave you. I'll always be with you, forever and ever!"

The corners of her tired mouth turned upward, as she repeated,
"We'll be together forever and ever, and we'll be . . . together!"
"Yes, Mom–forever and . . .", but she was gone in muffled snores.

Mom was in a hospital bordered by rugged mountains west of Ashland,
    Oregon,
almost overlooking steep cliffs, the crashing surf below.

13

I was driving Victoria, my 9-year-old; she had come all the way from Paris to
    see her.
As the car climbed a narrow road near Cave Junction,
a grey plateau of solid rock loomed before us.
We both got the idea the same time. Let's check it out!!

I parked the car. We followed a narrow dirt path winding upwards, in a gradual
    curve.
I headed first and Victoria followed.
Minutes later, a shrill scream curdled my soul.

I flew to her side
to see blood streaming down her face
from a red spot on her forehead,
as a wily brownish-grey snake slithered between two rocks above,
its rattles last.

I grabbed my screaming child as I cried . . . and trembled violently,
in the grasp of Hell.
But I had to keep calm and suck the poison.
She pushed me away, but I held fast, my mouth obstinately sucking,
covering the wound.

After spitting several mouthfuls of poison, slimed with blood
my baby's bellows had turned to whimpers, then . . . silence.
She was unconscious!
I held her as I slid down the side of the rock, my rear scraping . . . didn't feel it
and flew to the car.

It was an hour's drive, at winded speed, burning rubber,
barely making the curves
until I reached the nearest hospital, where my mother lay.
I stayed with Victoria the rest of the day and night,
only leaving her for a couple of minutes to climb the stairs to my mother's
    room
to tell her we'd be late—Victoria was a little sick.

In the morning, my loving daughter,
in spite of my frantic attempts to suck the poison away,
was declared brain dead.
I looked to her calm face, golden strands of hair
sticking to her slightly olive skin,
beneath the tubes, the tubes, the tubes.
Then cascades of tears
as I stood helpless . . . shivering . . . depleted
next to her bed.

I visited mom who was pale, lying there with oxygen prongs resting in her
    nose.
She could still smile, but her spirit was drifting . . . drifting

I took a motel room.
The hospital had refused my pleas to stay there,
trading off staying with my daughter and mother,
sleeping in a chair or on the floor, I didn't care.
No was the unfeeling, rule-driven answer.

The room was at a wayside motel, the sign drooping under a grey sky.
Shuttled the whole next day from one room to the other,
lavishing caresses, holding hands, leaving the room as warm springs welled and
    rose,
without release
I couldn't breathe but didn't want to.
Kept going . . .
Had to keep going . . .

I went downstairs to drink a cup of coffee— and think.
Then returned to Victoria's room.
Late that night was the changing of the guard.
I noticed a lag when nobody was around.
An idea, as I sat next to her stillness, scattered with wispy breaths

I decided . . .
    decided to take my loving family with me on a trip.

I sneaked into Mom's room when the nurses were on break
turned the light on and her eyes opened.
She nodded as I disconnected all the machines
to prevent an alert to the nurses' station.
I disconnected the oxygen, the IV, the tubes intubating her.
She knew . . .

I gathered her in my arms and lifted her up.
Reaching around her I sat her up in bed,
and brought in the wheelchair.
Weak, she tried to help me as I grunted and twisted,
getting her positioned.
I slowly pushed her out the door,
into the elevator,
then the car.

I returned, climbed the stairs to Victoria's room.
Peering down the hall, nobody stirred.
I returned to my baby, unplugged all the life support machines
disconnected the tubes and wires . . .

Kissing my little one, she took her last fleeting breaths.
Her lungs swelled and receded,
then stilled.
I gathered her into my arms.
Holding back my shakiness, a muffled cough escaped
My body shook involuntarily. as my eyes welled up.
But I wiped the tears on my shirt,
I strained to close my eyes to dam them, helping me focus.
As I tiptoed down the stairs, out the door
and laid her in the back seat.

As I drove my two loves, the northwestern wind blew
through the open windows.
I held my Mom's hand, stuttered while telling her
Victoria was sleeping in the back
but would soon rise to give her a big kiss . . .

"What's wrong, Frankie?" she asked, barely audible.
"Just tired, Mom. I love you."
And she nodded, her voice fading, "I love you."

Out of the corner of my eye, I saw her slump against the seat . . . and knew . . .
she was gone.
My body trembled; I jammed my finger between my teeth,
and opened the window. Tears blurred my eyes and my nose ran.
Couldn't breathe—stopped the car, looking straight ahead.
Couldn't look . . . couldn't look.

We arrived at the motel in about 20 minutes.
I gently held my baby in my arms—my Victoria—
took her to the room, laid her stiffening body on a bed.
I returned for Mom, rolled out the wheelchair stashed in the trunk.
Struggling, I twisted, finally heaved her out of the seat
into her wheelchair, one last time . . .

I pushed her to the room
slid her gently onto the other bed
and returned to lock and bolt the door.

I sat in between the beds, holding their hands
Tears gushing, torrential—
lost,
not knowing what to do, where to go.
I somehow fell asleep . . .

The piercing wail of distant sirens yanked me awake.
I looked out the window to see two police cars approaching, red lights whirling,
sirens shattering the crisp Oregon night.

One last long, loving kiss
on the cheeks of my beloveds,
I slipped out the back door, locking it behind me,
and walked—
walked toward the steep, jagged Oregon cliffs,

soaring bastions in the dark of a raw, northwestern evening.
I could see the glint of fierce, unbridled breakers
forming over the freezing sea
white foam of restless, swirling sea crashing below.
I gave a last look back to the police lights spinning 'round
 in front of the motel.

Walking out over the farthest cliff,
I glanced down as my pounding heart masked the sound of the waves
but the salt air whisking in the distant crashing,
reminded me they were there,
out there somewhere, at the edge
of a monstrous sea . . . in the blackness.

I looked one last time to the window of the room where my beloved ones lay;
 heard the door splinter as it was hammered down.
I stepped out on the ledge,
and launched my eager frame into black, waiting arms
and mysteriously, magically. . . time froze.

As I sliced through the thick, billowy cold wind,
I saw a stage lit up before me,
and Victoria performing "Singing in the Rain," before an enlightened crowd,
her red lips opening in an ecstatic smile.
Her brilliant smile—
She looked right at me in the crowd, right into my black eyes, peering out from
    inky depths . . .

I dropped deeper into the darkness, touching into another time and place.

I saw a beach lit up in the distance. It was Miramar,
a little nook along the Mediterranean,
next to Cannes, near the Riviera.
There I sat next to my mother
sipping cocktails, resting and dreaming together.
Cocktail in one hand, her hand in the other, looking over the aquamarine crests,
with her at my side gazing at me, through azure moons . . .

As I plummeted to the restless sea, the words came back–
they came back

"You'll be with me forever and ever . . . You'll be with me forever."

END

Frank Romano, New York City, August 2014

(Read by author at the 6th Edition of "From Whitman to Ginsberg: Subversive Poems that Challenge Conventional Wisdom", formerly entitled "The Anti-Tea Coffeehouse Poetry Collective". Cornelia Street Cafe, New York City, September 27, 2013. YouTube: https://www.youtube. com/watch?v=ABmdmxbgxrw)

Drone

The face off
Got to gut up . . .
But the changing shape of war
no face off
and no guts.

Now, just
    push a button
    and time explodes
    innocents are erased . . .
    massacred.

No inquiry . . . just
    turn off the machine
    and walk away
    shielded by constitutional rights.
    By corporate interests?

Don't fret
    but you're trembling with frustration
You're looking frenzied,
feathers ruffled in all four corners.
Tortured by impotent rage.

Wipe away your tears.
Wipe them—come on!

Oh, and sorry, but . . .
your phone's bugged.

No more leaders
Just shells

Politicians, like drones
 No eye-to-eye
 Controlled by blind ambition
 No compassion, and
 No heartbeat,

 inside.

Frank Romano, New York City, August 2013

(Read by author at the 6th Edition of "From Whitman to Ginsberg: Subversive Poems that Challenge Conventional Wisdom", formerly entitled "The Anti-Tea Coffeehouse Poetry Collective". Cornelia Street Cafe, New York City, September 27, 2013. YouTube: https://www.youtube.com/watch?v=ABmdmxbgxrw)

Squirrel

Something in the road
I slow
Tail
then peaked chin
Slow
    worried button eyes
I brake
    Black dots looking into mine
forlorn, like the cold hand of fog.

Then I see
Grey squirrel
crouches over
a flattened mass of hair, brown dust
Run over
Crushed
Laid out on the cold asphalt

My car creeps forward
The black dots again, then a tail flitting nervously
The flattened remains
    Once jumping in the trees, sliding down the trunk
    Squirrel love hidden in deep burrows
    In the trees, in the dark . . . squirrels chattering to each other
    warming the dark, humid burrow,
Now cold, stone cold
Still, silenced lover

The black paw, tail twitching
Tiny paw
    It can't be!
Pulling, trying to dislodge
the dried-up carcass, now embedded in the road

I stop the car again

As a branch falls next to the grey fury, the desperate lover
doesn't move an inch, pawing, scrapping, pulling, then sniffing
more pulling and sniffing
    The tangled lover scraping and pawing
    The black dots defiantly looking up, unblinking
  Lover's anguish

    Refuses to retreat,
  I yell, "Get out of the road!"
    Closer, I'm within a foot
    The paws reluctantly stop and
    the persistent grey lover withdraws into the shadows
    But not for long as my car has stopped
    a foot away from the downed animal
    I can no longer see the frantic lover
    But I distinctly hear
    Scraping, pulling,
    scraping, pulling
    Scraping . . . into the night

The grey phantom refuses to move,
before the heated radiator
    Undisturbed by the hoot of the owl overhead
    Scraping, pulling
    I back up about ten feet,
give them a wide berth and drive by

On the other side of the road
    the beloved grey companion gone
    The black dots, not looking up
    Frenzied scraping, pulling, scraping . . .

    God, I wish I could love like that!*

Dr. Frank Romano, New York City, 2015

* I feel my own deep love
and must not lose you
to know how profound it is.

Lance

About the author's Jewish American friend, Lance Wolf, a peace and freedom activist extraordinaire and a victim of being at the wrong place at the wrong time in Jerusalem. There, on August 18, 2010, two drunk youths took his life. But the author hopes Lance will be remembered since his legacy is now shared with you, the reader.

I never thought I'd be doing this—
writing a poem about you.

Because I assumed you'd always be here,
in this place, where tears glisten
long after the last hoopoe
has sung its sad melody
in the dim evening light
of Ibrahim's guest house
here,
in the Mount of Olives.

I miss you!
So desperate to feel your presence,
that this night
I had to write this or perish,
overflowing with grief.

****

The first thing I remembered
was your ranting and raving
your clarion calls,
questioning all my comfortable beliefs,
people I had blindly believed in.

I was an Obama apologist
until

you wiped my arguments away
with revelations of his incompetence,
broken promises, kowtowing to Israel,
to capitalist interest groups,
abandoning closure
of the ignominious Guantanamo Bay,
disastrous Middle East foreign policy,
his power and money hunger . . .

All that I had previously chosen to ignore.

So, you became the first and the last
person I turned to:
A litmus test, for everything—
from Israeli-Palestinian relations,
my peace and freedom demonstrations,
to the infamous Jewish settlers,
and the Palestinian Authority traitors
assisting the Israeli persecutors,
like the Vichy brown shirts collaborating with
the Nazis in France, during WWII—

your wisdom pulled me to earth,
and even helped me resolve my complicated
women problems . . . everything!

Your fervent desire for peace and freedom,
your love of humanity and hate of double-talking,
bribe-taking, self-interested politicians
and the pro-settler, ethnic cleansing
inflicted by the Israeli government
on Palestinians in the West Bank and Gaza . . .
all of this helped fuel my freedom marches.

What I most needed was accurate info
lots of it,
especially as an activist in this place,

the ever-changing Holy Land.
You were always there with sensitive thoughts,
open views, unshackled by rules.
Love you, guy!
Need you . . .

You'd be waiting for me downstairs,
the cool morning breeze
wafting gently through your wiry brown hair,
white on the fringes,
while drinking your tea.

Slightly bent over the corner table,
you'd be munching on Kmaj bread,
in the kitchen,
shaggy white moustache drooping over
tight, narrow lips,
scraggly beard
covering chin and neck
hints of light brown embedded in white.

I would saunter in,
with eyes half closed
after morning prayers and meditations,
failing to completely recoup
from the day before,
the demonstrations for peace and freedom
in the West Bank.

You would hand me a cup of strong Palestinian coffee,
your flaming hawk eyes following my hand
as it reached out,
then jumping to my eyes.
A subtle twitch flattening the top of your eyes
meant a smile that your mouth didn't reflect.
But I knew. That was your way!

After quickly downing the strong coffee
with a liberal dose of grounds,
I would stuff bread soaked with olive oil
and dipped in za'atar
into my mouth, and
before the grounds had time to settle,
we'd hug . . . for eternity.

As I made my way to the door,
you'd always say, "Be careful!"
quite facetiously,
before I plodded back to the Damascus Gate,
then to the West Bank
or Jerusalem's Old City,
for demonstrations, interfaith events,
for freedom, for life.

Sometimes even in the face of Kalashnikovs,
    Palestinian collaborators, the
M16's of Israeli soldiers, or tear gas—
unlimited arms and weapons—paid for by
US tax dollars . . .

Harassment, arrest and detention,
Sometimes dragged away from the ruthless occupiers,
by Palestinian doctors and ambulance drivers,
who quickly patched me up,
even stitched me with sewing thread
or slapped an oxygen mask
on my hacking, sputtering mouth . . .

But nothing compared to my friend,
Juliano Mer-Khamis,
another activist extraordinaire,
who courageously, with his mother Arna,
founded the "Freedom Theatre"
in the Jenin refugee camp.

Who took five shots of steel to the gut,
through a window of despair,
and perished seated in a car,
his baby son on his lap . . .

Turning back to you, in the open door,
before I lumbered down the stairs
to the small passage leading to the street below,
I'd turn to you saying, "You're in the trenches;
you live here, my friend, every day. You're the one!"

 As I walked to the Arab bus,
 a couple of blocks away,
during my last stay at Ibrahim's,
while you were still alive,
I mumbled to myself, thinking of you,
"You incredible crackpot! You dared
to speak even the ugly truth,
not fearing to yell explosively
in the middle of a room
filled with bobble-headed Jewish peaceniks!
You challenged them, their hypocrisy of
crying brotherhood with Palestinians while
still supporting the cruel occupation,
the treacherous confiscation of Palestinian lands,
the brutal blockade of Gaza,
all with a smile!"

You sometimes didn't make sense, with
your crazy bellowing.
But you do, now, more than ever!

Stepping into the street, I was greeted by
the usual clanking madness of honking horns,
intertwining with a myriad street peddlers,
Palestinian youth playing soccer,
girls wearing their multi-colored head scarfs,

returning from school.
Cars whizzing by, near the bus stop,
near Salman Al-Farse Street,
where I stood, waiting for my ride
to Jerusalem's Old City
where Al-Aqsa and
Dome of the Rock mosques loomed;
the Western Wall had witnessed
centuries of wailing;
where Jesus had carried the cross
to his crucifixion.

Down the stretch, I looked for a bus,
but none in sight.
One finally poked through the maze of vehicles
and jaywalkers coming from the other side,
bearing down on me.
Stopping next to me with a slight screech,
I climbed the stairs.
After a "Salaam alaikum" and dropping 5 shekels
into the waiting hands of the driver,
I was in . . . and on my way to Hebron.

They labelled me crazy,
during my ranting and raving
demonstrations on the Hebron streets that day . . .
When I returned to Ibrahim's place,
you were standing next to the door
with a wrinkled brow,
and placing a hand on my shoulder,
you grumbled,
"Got to talk with you."
You had obviously already heard about Hebron.
I cringed, waiting for harsh words,
that I had done something wrong again:
Another blasphemy desecrating

the sacred soil of this religious labyrinth.

Instead, your wrinkled brow smoothed over
when you laughed and said,
"Now we've got something in common!"

You always supported me because
you believed in me, as
I believed in you . . . always.
But you're dead!

And I still hear your words, "Be careful . . ."

Well, for you—for you—I'll make sure
 I'm not careful!!! Not anymore . . . that's over!

In my comfort zone of illusions and delusions,
you helped to strip them away.

But you're not around, Bro,
to hug.

****

The next morning,
I lay in my sleeping bag,
with these words scribbled on a piece of paper
slightly crumpled and splotched
with yesterday's coffee grounds
the air pungent with cardamom, the spicy
scent of the Arab world.

Muezzins from the 4 corners of Jerusalem
began echoing their pleas to come and pray,
as the first light blazed over the distant hills.

I got up and glanced out my window

The morning dew shimmered in the trees
Haze shrouded the Mount of Olives.

The steam was rising,
curling over your tweed moustache

Because your face is there . . . it's there . . .

Frank Romano
Mount of Olives, Jerusalem, September 2010

Across the Gulf of Sorrento

When the author was visiting a friend in Sorrento, Italia, he looked out over the Golfo di Sorrento to Naples, the source of his Italian roots. He imaged his grandfather and grandmother dreaming of America and after mustering up enough courage and money, making the voyage in a ship. He was so moved viewing the birthplace of his Italian family roots, he wrote this poem, starting in Sorrento and finishing it as his bus arrived in Napoli, before taking the plane back to Paris, France.

A wind plays to the heart

> of a lonely beach
> Lonely beach . . .

Like the grapes you held out to me,

as you dreamed of America
> with deep chocolate eyes,[1]
> gazing over the sugar
> coating the crusty shell of the brioché

You gawk at open truths

Crossed the ocean
you took me there
Touch of a baker man[2]

---

[1] Referring to Romano's Grandparents on my Father's side, both born and raised in Napoli.

[2] Romano's grandfather, Francesco Romano, a Napolitano, (born in Napoli) was a baker after he was released from Ellis Island, New York. He then lived in New York City—probably in the Bronx—and then probably Brooklyn and at some time, apparently lived in Chicago. Then, part of the family moved to Providence, Rhode Island, and to Walpole, Massachusetts, near Boston.

painting from long brushes
you never saw
Caruso's breath whispered

of a lonely beach,
Lonely beach . . .

But when the mist rose
there was Napoli,

And you drew in a silent breath

Crossed the ocean
you took me there
Touch of a baker man
painting from long brushes
you never saw

With makeup powder clouding the air about you
with every soaring leap, Caruso y mio nono[3]
dancing over the Amalfitano Cliffs,
I could not reach you

as you dreamed of America
with deep chocolate eyes,
gazing over the sugar
coating the crusty shell of the brioché

In your womb, mia nona
your eyes blinked
Only those creamy bright Mediterranean eyes
they dropped so
on the beach that night

---

[3] Caruso again, with makeup during a performance, this time dancing with Romano's Grandfather. Enrico Caruso, born in Naples, was one of the greatest opera singers.

Lonely beach,
    lonely beach . . .
then rose to fly across the Atlantico,
And in the end,
your deep chocolate eyes closed, just closed[4]

bringing everyone blinking into your womb[5]

    Blinking for you, Nona
    Blinking for you . . .

Crossed the ocean
you took me there
Touch of a baker man
painting from long brushes

you never saw.

Frank Romano
Sorrento & Napoli, Italia, June 2013

---

[4] Referring to Romano's Grandmother's death; she was Napolitana, (born in Napoli). Her maiden name was Fatima Gallucci.

[5] Romano's grandmother had complications after giving birth to his father, in Providence, Rhode Island. Romano believed she had other health issues and died either giving birth to his father or not long afterwards.

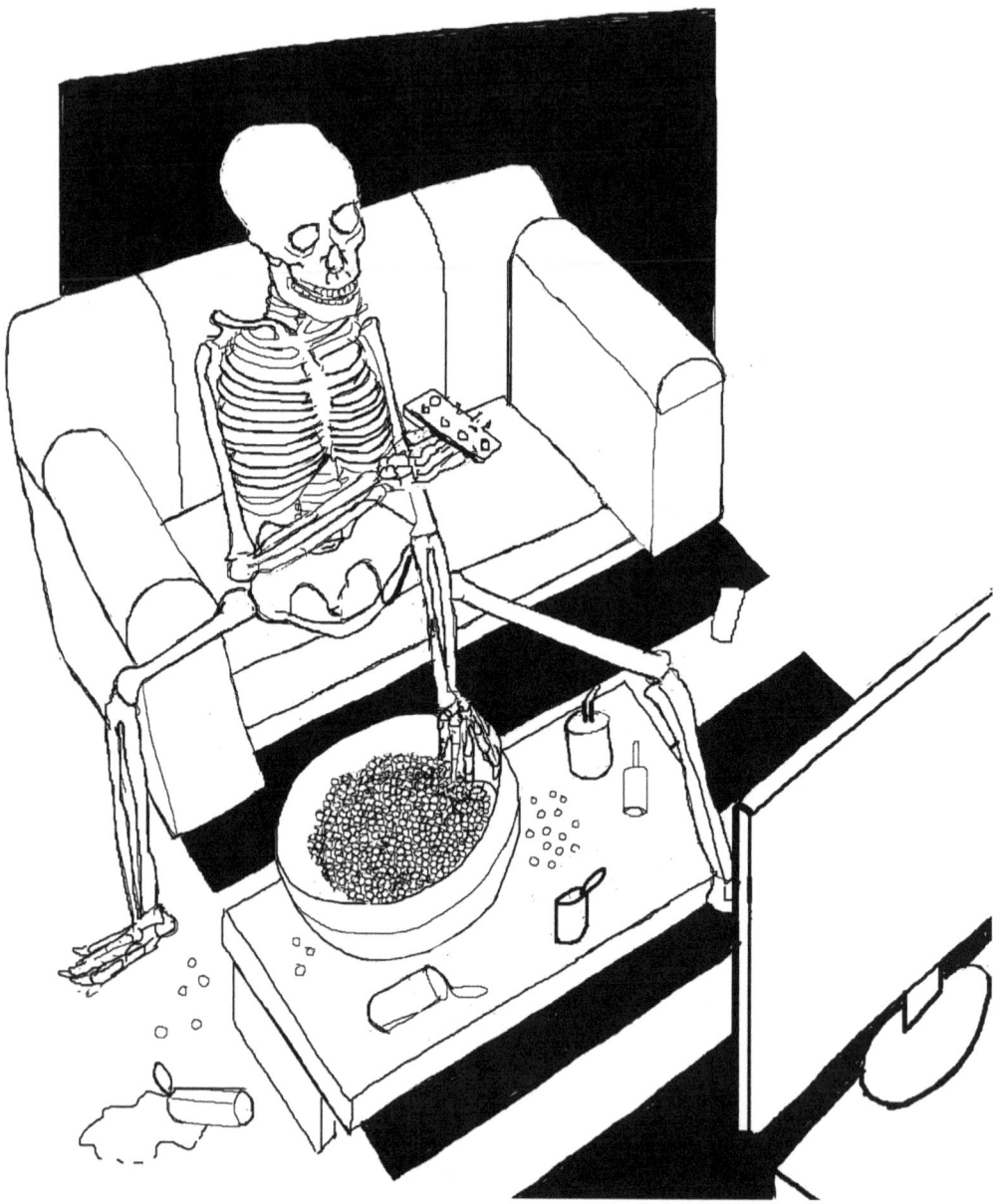

Bread & Gladiators

Just wanted to talk
    just . . . talk
Close
Feels vacuous
How do you feel?
But
just
not
you.
You talked 49ers, yardage,
Your team . . .
But what about you? Your life?
You said,
Bad scene, like the movie "The Shining"
    Like crazed Nicholson
    When Wendy finds the manuscript
    "All work and no play . . ."
Not you, not me
Always somebody else.

Like you don't matter, don't exist
Not me, not you?
I ask you about your love—silence. Instead, you say,
"No—Madonna's new lover!"
What about your baby? Yoooooour baby? Wow!
No? No, you tell me. Not yours?
Kardashian's new baby?
Just name dropping, 24/7?

But your success, your creations, your challenges?
Yes, yes!
No, no . . . you say Manning, at the super bowl
becomes a hero . . .

Bread and gladiators
But I—me—I . . . I want to play . . .
    not be stuck on the bench,
Not be somebody else's cheerleader
For the rest of my life.

No, and
I don't want Julia Roberts, Meryl Streep
DiCaprio, the talented illusionists—
Actors glorified far more than the real people they play—
To live my dream, following a script.
Illusions now mean more than reality??

I only want you . . .
just you.

What? Living by proxy?
Yeah, I know: life's become so linear, monotonous
Cool technology brings static conformity
Machines think and maybe soon, will even FEEL
for us? Like in the movies?
Canned emotions on the silver screen.
 And we now live the movies? Sports? The media?

And you say technicity, high tech, state of the art
means perfection,
And I say, not perfection, but a way
to control us, placate us.
Send us into a mindless stupor
stacked in front of the screen.

Bread and gladiators . . . bread and games
To stifle your voice in an artificial,
sterile comfort zone.
A computerized life passionless distance,
virtual and
. . . minimal. . .

The staff of a meaningless life.
Bloated like
spectator popcorn bred in machines,
More hot air than substance
Like automatons
Manipulated, overridden
marinated in
      a lifetime of illusions.
Eyes that never blinked.

Bread and games
But you don't question
As you watch your films
jump up and down
In the stands
Safe, comfortable, noncommittal.

Now getting older
Bread and games
Except for stashing cars, houses, toys, things
in a box labeled "My Success,"
What have we done? What did we do?

But it's only a box kicked between the uprights—
a field goal kicked . . . always by someone else, again,
while loafing and cheering, at
the Bread and games

But now life is almost over
Go sweep all your THINGS into
the middle of the arena,
the amphitheater of someone else's fight
Go ahead!

And there you are on the silver screen,
at "The End"—stiff, cadaverous,
sitting in the middle of the field
with a glacial, hollow smile
as the light pierces through
your empty body.

Frank Romano
Paris, February 2016

(Bread & Gladiators refers to the practice of Roman emperors of handing out free wheat to poor Roman citizens as well as providing entertainment, such as gladiatorial games.

In a <u>political</u> context, it refers to the Roman emperors attempts to generate public approval, especially by the poor masses, by offering a <u>palliative</u> to them: for example food (bread) and entertainment (circuses). Bread & gladiators is a derivative of a commonly used phrase "bread & circuses," which refers to a palliative offered in particular to appease the masses and avoid potential discontent.

In the poem, the author likens the palliative of bread & gladiators to movies, television programs, video games, etc., forms of entertainment that "feed" and perhaps distract our minds from seeking who we are, what our true passion is, and what we need to do to live it in order to find self-fulfilment and true happiness.)

Gunned Down?

The night after the author had organized a Peace & Freedom demonstration in Jenin, West Bank, Israeli soldiers stormed the Jenin Refugee Camp to arrest a Palestinian youth accused of terrorist activities. He was shot and killed. The next day, the author was prevented from leaving Jenin, due to a riot by Palestinians protesting the killing of their compatriot the night before. During the uprising, however, something magical happened, as portrayed in the following poem.

Did you gun me down?
in the camps tonight?

Four thin shadows bedded under the stars
An explosion shook the rickety timbers
of the overgrown hut
and the helmeted shouts wake up
Bang--and a boy went down

Did you gun me down?

The next day, on the way to the shuttle,
my return ride to Jerusalem,
I watched on the sidewalk
a wild, red-eyed mob
winding around the town, circling the block, invading the street . . . hordes
some carrying Islamic Jihad flags,
some shooting off AK-47's into the sweltering heat,
others breaking bottles and ramming their fists into shop windows.

The Palestinian Police had disappeared —avoiding clashes, I was told.
The boys–hundreds–invaded the streets. I couldn't move, stuck alongside,
watching my shuttle
head to Jerusalem without me, on the other side.
Tires were ignited, dirty rubber smoke infused the air, singeing my throat.

43

Did you gun me down?

Then, something strange . . .
The chaotic, frenzied mob turned the corner
and about 50 boys turned, pointed at me,
started walking, then running towards me.

Will you crush me down?

I flashed on what an out-of-control mob could do
Too late!
I cringed; no time to pray—too shocked to pray.
Tight lips, then smiles and then . . .
they seemed to lift their thumbs in unison
I thought for the governor's assistant, standing next to me
but the boys ignored him . . . and appeared to be looking at me.

I was then surrounded by them,
but instead of grabbing me
they were lining up, reaching out to shake my hand.
I shook their outstretched ones, dumbfounded, with eyes brimming over
Blurred images
I wasn't harmed . . .

I didn't get it!
Then, as if a horn had called them,
they returned, almost running backwards, were reabsorbed into the
stampeding hordes.

Why didn't you crush me down?

Something had happened.
And then I remembered the eyes of the youth leader
heading towards me.

His eyes told me—flaming red eyes
that softened when they settled on mine.

They told me . . .
told me . . .

Frank Romano, Jenin, West Bank, Palestine, September 2013

(Read by author at the 6th Edition of "From Whitman to Ginsberg: Subversive Poems that Challenge Conventional Wisdom", formerly entitled "The Anti-Tea Coffeehouse Poetry Collective". Cornelia Street Cafe, New York City, September 27, 2013. YouTube: https://www.youtube.com/watch?v=ABmdmxbgxrw)

Walk with ME
(Last Poem to You—)

You've come through again . . . Spirit
showing me wisdom in
the mist, spreading over distant hills
like Southern Oregon hands,
cradling me,
But then comes a clutching
My love . . . deeper than the grey seas
An illusion?

Walk with me

Listening to the creek—creamy mountain springs
over smooth rock
And telling me I was wrong
Love wasn't there—
contrived by my lonely heart
Never mind . . .

Walk with me

For the wisdom in my heart
told me so
The love wasn't there.

Walk with me, then

Arm in arm
In deep forest, humid bonds
where you became a dark-grey trunk
looming solid—there for me
in your course, rough-hewn garb—steadfast
Not like your fleeting heart
grasping onto purchased passions

but not onto me,
And not free . . .

Walk with me

Tell me true:
Was it all
a lie?
But I forgive you, I—I forgive you
for not ripping your heart from your
bosom, protected,
As I did from mine, exposed,
to give you . . .

But you turned away . . .
SHHHH   SHHHHH SHHHHHHHHHHHHHH
Just . . .
Walk with me

Frank Romano, Ashland, Oregon, October 2012

Festival of Life

The hopes of all will create love
with tidings of a new world, new life...
The beauty of a single grape leaf
representing purity, green, a succulent morsel.
The lone Dionysus is wandering near
he may be dancing with the sun through the trees
or gossiping with inquisitive pigeons around the bend.
Suddenly, inhabitants of the forest come out to play
everyone dances to the beat of the winded trees
bright colors flash as nature swings
food is passed from paw to hand
birds drink nectar from an earthen cup,
everyone gathers to hear the beat of a faraway song
then silence as if nothing happened.
The wind is quiet, the leaves are still, not a sound.
But if you concentrate on the air
love vibrations are faintly felt,
made by soft steps of the Festival of Life.

San Francisco, 1970

Over the Line

I crossed the line—
passions streamed from my fingertips
I crossed the line
touching your soft face
that I had held so dear
for so many moments

I crossed over
life and death no longer have meaning
endless searching for sanity
because I crossed over
into pure amor—
to touch you again
    And die

because I crossed over
into my tears of longing
I crossed over—never more to return
to a controlled existence—
    it is no longer possible
        in the reflection of your eyes
           in the puddle
                leading up to a place
      where we touched—
      our hearts so interweaving
      so out of breath, gasping—

So, I crossed over
never to return
from a correct life
socially acceptable
flirting with emotional, mental disaster
upon every breath
that I shall ever take
I will—cross over
    To your love.

San Francisco, 2004

Empty Passion

It's hell—hell by the bottom of soul's torment
trying to make out a meaning
lighting the bureaucracy's false blessing
security—weakness
"a foolish consistency is the hobgoblin of little minds"
Emerson's words constantly hitting me constantly warning me
blessing the sad but live warmth of the solidarity I feel
I expecting nothing
living intensely among passion's mixed triumph
of confidence and indecision—
yet, the meaning endures
for once living for principles
deeply ingrained in the soft touch of a mother's shroud
and Dad's life embrace of endless cold
trying to breathe life in a strobe-lit dancy-flirty
superficial world where essence is reversed
        and passions are repressed in the name of progress.

Paris, 1978

Cosmic Light

Let me
allow
my thoughts
to flow
into the blueness of
sky—
with faith
naturally—
feeling of strength
sometimes of
weakness
with faith
embrace
me
with love
I understand
and
I will
seek to understand
in your love
and seek a better
world
and not force life.
Let it flow
into the warm water
of your
caressing light.

San Francisco, 1990

Simplicity

Living—for money—
seeing—for television
thinking—for technology

Why in the maze of all things are values
distorted to please
the very earth-shaking murmurs of existence?

and pleasures are planned.

Brussels, 1979

Mediterranean

Dreaming about the cool breeze
wafting foam riding abreast the wave
upon my face in the impassioned grasp of
the Mediterranean—

caressing with voluptuous Italian waves
holding me close to my ancestor's bosom
The Mediterranean—spontaneous laughter
inward warmth rising to the surface
in the shape of a smile—
this is where I belong
this is my home—thousands of miles from the cradle
of my birth
I still have the warm water flowing through
my veins

I salute you, Mediterranean, from the coast of Spain
to the flaming shores of Italy,
the white sands of Israel to the Egyptian beaches,
to the rolling dunes of Morocco
the cool caressing waves
deep blue eyes mystifying the desire
to passionately grasp the tips of the smooth waves
hurl hearts of lovers
floating on the crest of the old world
and renewing its strength as the new world
embraces nurtured traditions
red-blue explosive adrenalin popping
mystical blue
vibrating from the inner womb of the
Mediterranean.

Campo Amor, Spain, 1986

Held You

You were born there
In that place
You were in my arms there

Fighting for your breath
    Your head—angular

Gleams of hope

Empuja a la vida (push to life)

You did it
We did it

We revived
    My dead son
Fetus without a chance

A doctor's fleeting choice

    Your life leaking out

With the doctor's distracted voice

But I held you

    My still born

And I love you,

    But from me you're torn

Paris, 2008

Pa

Pa, weak
but alive—
let me breathe
into you
my strength
to make you whole
not all of it, as
I shall surely die—
but take half of it
I'll do fine.
take one of my lungs,
or one of my legs
I'd do anything
to keep you strong—
Cut my heart in two
I'll divide my heart with you

there's plenty left to love

I'd give you one eye
if you could no
longer see the
deep blue sky
in your eyes—
reflecting ma's
never-ending battle
to hold onto life
your love
of yesteryear

and for all times
from youth
to old age—
forever love
'til the end,
And far beyond.

Paris, 2004

City

What did it feel like?
To be in love
Us two
In the city

Running from building to building
Searching for tenderness
Caring
Trying not to play the games

But playing them anyway
I stopped to think
How lucky I was
You were here

To share the masked
face of the city
quick minds and fast tempers
Where the money flowed

Where the street people scratched
looking for scraps of food
in the garbage
leaning over, busily rummaging

You chased the lonely spirit from me
lurking—
bouncing from one side of the street
to the other

We weathered it
but our time had come
to flee and refresh
the wayward heart palpitated again-

Breaking from the clotted rut
that we were getting into

Yet the warmth of your being
is missed

So missed—that I imagine you are here
sometimes-next to me
Just to make me feel secure again

Are you there?
Next to me
holding my hand
telling me . . .

it's OK.

San Francisco, 1983

The Race Track

All I can offer the world
Is that which the world seldom values-
My heart.

others laugh—
because they feel that their life
is valued
according to what they produce,
by their work, good fortune or both

So, they terminate their lives
measured in dollars.

A horrible thought,
To value something as priceless
as a life, with all the emotions and
passions—
they say that love can be reduced to the flesh
that from which offspring are generated

The love for one's parents, mates, friends,
Kids, where does that go—after death—
on a racetrack revolving around
the odds?

San Francisco, 1986

Droplets on a Blade of Grass

Droplets spot a dangling blade of grass—
enthralling me with the wildest of dreams—
that I have rejoined the earth
and am no longer bludgeoned by lies—
no more fighting for principles—
the only principles that remain—
are:
the droplets that spot a dangling blade of grass—
surrounded by a warm humid smell
in the country pastures in la Sarthe—
pastures fed by mother's agents—
fallen oaks and layers of grass—blended in
the kaleidoscope of seasons' tints
and mama's pies caste in morning flowers—
only to be greeted by:

the droplets spotting a dangling blade of grass.
blissful nature entreating me to
withdraw from the lonely
and entwine my swollen eyes around
a dried up old tree trunk surrounded by
droplets that spot a dangling blade of grass.

Paris, 1979

Obliged

No!
I
will do
as I
feel,
passionately
breathing
fire
into
the air
love's trembling
fountain-ing
forth
creative
spasms
alive
living
living
alive
living
refusing
to
descend
into
the
depths
of
illusion
that
is made
whole
upon
submitting

to
society's
pressures
to
accumulate
to
materialize
to
consume
to
consume
to
hate
to
abuse
to
arm
to
demonstrate
physical
    prowess
to disintegrate.

San Francisco, 1987

But the Silence

One lives for nature's invites,
Causing, during each particular part,
The flowing of all the fish toward deeper seas-
When the silent river begins to dry-
Yet the key to-a-rebirth-an awakening-
is not the changes the waters keep question-less—
but the silence-

Look to thyself, the prophet calls out before death-
And they look to the kings and queens of flash-
And dance and flash and dance and flash-
Dance to saxophone wails, sax dance, sax dance-
And you have to repeat that which truly is the same-
Except the silence

Speak to me father, speak to me mother, sister brother-
I can't stand the silence-
Yet when we speak-vision TV bulbs dancing
With the story guided by dreams and dreams,
But the silence

And I am calmed-
Pieces of dreams are glued together
Sleep is consumed-all drifts together-
But the silence

And now in searching-secure falters-
As crystal shines a pinpoint of light-fading
But the silence

Your majesty, lord garage keeper, you are the same together-
But the silence
But the silence
But the silence.

Ashland, 1981

The Complete Journey

At night, the street reflects melancholy spirits
silent, doomed with passions
and the mournful street lamps
pave the way to my thoughts.

Strolling along an avenue of quiet frustration
I become limp of all feeling
and let the moon guide me along
to the banks of a cavernous great lake
with shadows of scary depth

I am afraid to draw near to
because unknown damp lakes
with spongy bottoms
are disguised as harmless caverns
in which a death-ness prevails

and smooth bodies of spirited mist
slender, settle upon the cold surface
somewhere in that dark
forbidden world of fear.

No, I won't draw near.
I am pretending that
evil spirits lurk there
and I must seek what's up ahead.

There--at last I have found it,
the other side of the lake
from whence I started.

Santa Rosa, 1968

False Poets

Poet
what does that mean
"pretentious fool"?

Hibernating
in the cafes
in the
streets
you are
but
a tourist.

San Francisco, 1983

Urge to Tomorrow

War is
now.

Need to
think
to feel
but this
terrible
battle
consumes
me.

I,
I want to
live
tomorrow.

Yesterday I
lived for
tomorrow
but I got
nailed,
almost coffin
lid
shut
so, I picked
my-
self
up
and I
learned
when you
are in middle

of battle
win the battle
first
then think about
then think about
a little rest.

Can't think about
rest
'til the
bugle blows
'til the bugle blows.

San Francisco, 1987

Life

suburban
Crystal
Ball
Magic
life in a tube
in a box
surrounded by more boxes

competition to see
who has the biggest box-

or the brightest color
box—

let's see if you can
fit your Mercedes
in the box—

in which you lie
when you die

Maybe the
Box
will be
red.

San Francisco, 1987

Love

Is there but a little
tenderness
in the pleasure of your
womb
where you welcome
and then master
and then reject

Are you trying
to vindicate—

to sublimate revenge
for another
as you

ensnare
lonely
hearts
like mine—
if it weren't for
the raving Grace—
my love for unity
metaphysical yearning

I would be, yet
another
of
your
victims.

Paris, 1979

Conform

less problems
less feelings
safe
sure
assured
lasted
vacuum
empty

San Francisco, 1987

Numb

Choking
on the dust
of my own pretension

I realize
that
I'm trying too hard
to be cool

I'm living
for acceptance—
doing things
that aren't me

is it Ok, anyway
just because it feels cool?

that I forget
what it
tastes like
to be me.

to be free.

San Francisco, 1988

Freedom

Wind
breathing
into
me
filling my gills
shred of strength

That I
don't
need
to see
myself
in the
news
to know
I
exist.

Feeling of oneness
at a
different
level—
beyond
such
revival—
money
beyond
the gypsy lips
of stool pigeons

beyond envy—
to a plain

farther beyond
infinitely more
        beautiful....

Where our
Hearts
lie?

San Francisco, 1987

In Style

What's it now?
Curly hair, straight hair
red hair, blond hair—
earrings in the nose, in the lips—
don't matter man, it's cool.

It's cool do it, be cool
If you're not, you're out
So, let's get cool.

be fast, talk fast,
ride fast, drink fast—
Do it, it's cool—
it's on T.V. 'cuz it's cool
be it-be alive-!!

Just follow, come on—
Be fast, fast foods, fast rap
be cold-it's alright-be violet, be aggressive,
be punk, it's the new thing, new wave, it's in the movies
listen to the new songs.

Alright-man—
You're in—be conservative!
vote Nixon
vote Bush

Wow! Let's play war—
that's cool—
let's kill people—
in Central America
in South America—
in Vietnam—

in Iraq
in Palestine
'cause they aren't cool

Be yourself—
Oh man—no—
not that!!—that's not cool
Fall in love? Yeah, why not!
as long as it's cool!!

Paris, 2004

Dream with Me

Even
if life sometimes
pales
dream with me

that the little red flowers—
sitting on the side of the little hill
will bloom forever—
Just think, you and me
for an eternity
even though we're not together
dream with me

wherever you are
there is still that
mystical wave
throbbin' through us
whether we're aware
of it or not
our unique love is still there

Come with me
away
in a dream

San Francisco, 1982

Without Asking

Freedom to love you
demands its price—
to purchase a commitment

But—there is a flower
for every flower
there is a free person

cultivating the earth
around the moon
freedom to grow
without shrouds

But- constraining me to
conform,
to shape
life
in the form of a tree,
without asking the tree?

San Francisco, 1985

Stolen Heart

I don't search for motive-
because I have found it.
Motive is to unify all peoples
to spread warmth and love
to all who follow
Don't fear, my pretty little friend
no life is worth living unless it
can restore happiness, to a heart deflated.
But if you stop for motivation
don't let the crickets catch you stealing.

Santa Rosa, 1968

The River

Remember the river
that flows
so quietly
into the reservoir
of your embrace
and how the river
glistens
the light reflects
stories of all
the ages
and the sound
of water over
smooth rock
washing away
the tears
the red eyes
the tortuous
city blues
remember
time heals
and the river
is there
to remind
you.

Paris, 1980

Española Señorita

Midnight hair, smooth, lightning and
thick, neatly weaving down her sleek back,
sensuously titillating tender sheaths of skin on her
nude shoulder tanning in the sun simple,
taut, creamy, barbarous, copulational hair-receptive
but taut, gentle but restrained, magnificent but
simple. Moonish reflections on a "Black Tide"-the black tide
turns into a flaming mass of ravishing strands
searching serpents-each one destined to uncover an
unknown facet of innermost thought; the
moonish reflection still evident; yet the girl
disappears.

She walks with purpose,
Rhythmically fluctuates a higher stepping cadence
1-2-3-4, while the leg muscles blemish the smooth
consistency of her strong stacked legs-her head and
legs tense as the lioness stalking—her nose pointing
towards prey.

Her eyes are of a stray cat, receding and bent on fear,
virginous flurry, dark foreboding mysterious light floating, spinning,
twirling, aghast at the depths of her weary body-napkin
between flesh, and cavernous wombness and solitude-
searching, grasping, endlessly yearning for violent union;
pregnant, marriage, job, flight, buses, hitchhiking, walking
cussing, spitting, virginous flurries-get hitched so
to flee house, latched to a star-shining, burning, receding
fading, falling, faded.

Santa Rosa, 1973

Loneliness

Hopeless people in a hopeless world—
where money buys all—
even souls up for auction, my little pretty--
Dark French eyes glaring into mine
in a Mellaray Bar, near Chartre Cathedral—
we charm each other-
me from another world—from ghettos
to warm country homes and aged Victorians—
To you, the solid bourgeoisie, Paris 16th district
flashy smiles—latest threads heaving down
from your smooth neck—
and you—proudly wearing the dress
your papa bought you—
like a plastic orangutan smothering your last hope
for freedom
love is a 3-letter word—maybe 2 letters for short—
then just 1, just 1, just 1

Man without a cause—
the infernal tempest loathing and burning
fastidious fire breathing violent love
—like the wooden gates slamming.
But in the tender softness of a summer night
of a Northern California country town,
the dust wafting the fans of the overhead palm trees
my home among dirt-streaked hands
just honest love is all I ask.
Subtle strings of Cartesian passions
only mask the final glows
of purely simple desire—

before the disgruntled gloom
of forever sameness
of tombs' masked violence
their hinges glorifying nothing

dreaming, dreaming shifty speeds
splintering the essence on the cold pavement
too hard to caress my longings' covered mist
procreating illusions
before the endless torment and final
revelation where I am calmed by an
incredible optimism founded—fondly on the
soft shoulder you gave me
on which I rest my head full of unearthly
passions.
unearthly—ungodly—how dare me express my passions!
rage to live
passions for a simple love
                              I almost found.

Almost bending silent disturbed patterns
blissful remembrance of the tender
California nights where years of
regressive education erased itself.
We found understanding in the silence,
in the dark
and the simple murmur of the night bird
and the shadow of the leaves waving
in the breeze
outside the paned window
and the slow jazz of eternal savor,
perpetual love of
this moment preserved and perpetuated

Let it go and see it then
and breathe it into you—
before we self-destruct in the gifty-shifty
lightly endless patterns of billboards painted
in earnest salesmanship—

For my body and soul are throttled
by an army of invaders trying
to carry my soul away.

Paris, 1979

Almost Darlin'

Well, darlin'—your little white American cheeks-
full-faced-petite plump-grinning
darlin'—we must have passed each other a million times
"un coup d 'oeil"—a flick of an eye—
darlin' New York, city slickin' night crawlin'—
jumbo lovin'-somethin' in a gangster movie—
But your pale skin caressed me with a soft grin—
in the moonlight that we never shared—
not even in whispers—

Darlin'-but I know you honey—we never talked—
before you left, I told a friend, about you—
she's got the purtiest shoes—
you overheard me, and almost cried—
And the moonlight that we never shared
not even in whispers.

Paris, 1977

Passion

Battle of
free
the Spirit
beneath
the crusty ages of
time—
seeping through
pores of
forgotten—
dreams

San Francisco, 1988

Fear

Is the dastardly,
menace
waiting to greet you
at every turn—
For fear is a serious
enemy,
grasping, clawing, within
suction like claws
trying to clamp down on
the spiritual truth
of faith
which kills
fear
And love,
will guide my heart
leaving fear beside the
lonely, desolate meaningless
road
where it belongs.

Paris, 1978

Parisian Nights

A subtle light
Sifting through the silk curtains
Draped down over the tall stately windows
Of the Parisian bedroom
On the ground level—
Pretended passivity
From the quiet,
Masked the explosive
Rage
Trembling in earthly charges
And withdrawals
Crying out with tempest
In the Parisian night
Sweetened by a "baba au rhum" cake
Topped with fresh cream—
Inundated with the finest Jamaican rum—

Paris—
Never leave me—
Let me live thee
In all your creative delights
Sometimes drowning me in your
Philosophers, poets, artist

But Paris, don't leave me—
I need your will to survive—
Your radiant beauty embellishes with age
Proof of your survival—
And your expansive effervescence
Churning the petit prejudice
Into an honest, rage to be

Just Paris, but I left you
Only in body—
The smooth interior of your
         Caress—

Awaits me
In the familiar café near Odeon,
Or near St. Sulpice
Where I first tasted the ripeness of
Flaring passions—

In the early morning
As the pigeons danced on the ledges of the
Old Apartment building—
We were thrashing in lovers whispers—
As we possessed each other
So completely—
So primitively—
The magic is still in the air
The magic of spontaneous encounter
And opened expressions
And searching
For warmth
In the blue snow.

San Francisco, 1982

We Are

Seeds of the oak
flourishing
made of the same
inherited sperm
as mine
basking
in the sun
we are related
the trees
you
me
the earth
its deep rich smell
caresses my insides
after a cool rain
we are equal
you
me
the earth.

San Francisco, 1990

Return to the Living

Feeling

that life

has been sometimes

put on hold

to kick that button

out

Sometimes takes

All the strength

I've got.

Layaway feelings

surface

only when they are

traveling

in a desert.

San Francisco, 1983

Speed

In a hurry?

to buy a thing

to comb the streets

with feasting eyes

to consume

blasting through the crowds—

the end in sight?

jumping over curbs

middle of the night

weaving through the passersby

charging with all your might

chasing your tail

guarding your territory

for which you will readily fight

joining the crowd

advancing, hurrying

to get nowhere—
nowhere--

.

San Francisco, 1985

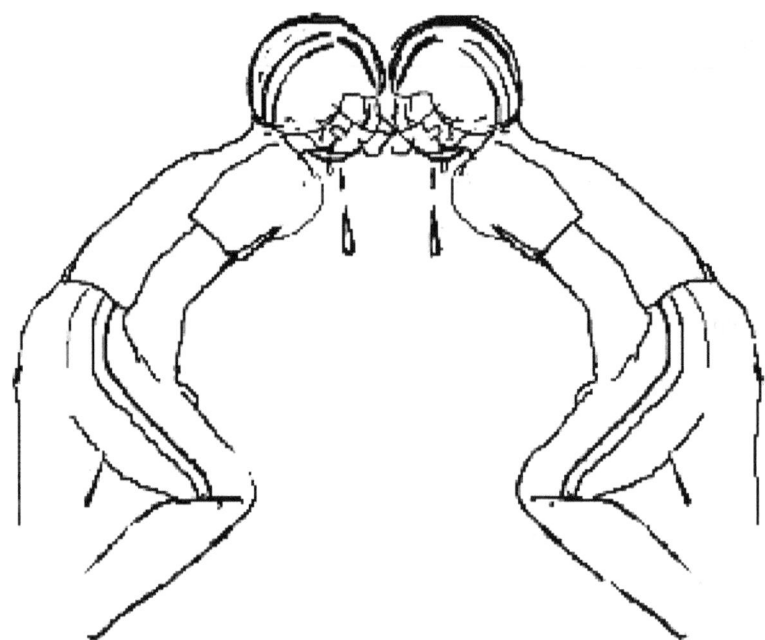

Fourth Quarter

Fighting a bitter battle
'til the end
body trembling,
worn out, burned up nerves
cringing at any mention
of battle
Yet again
into
the battle
trying to generate enthusiasm
from wasted limbs
singed nerves
with heart incessantly pumping
blood-streaked muddied jerseys
forgetting the wounds
to forge ahead
to the end
to the end.

Santa Rosa, 1986

Traces of Happiness

There is always a little truth in every man/woman relationship-
And then there is the time when emotions,
Surfacing spilling their endless sensations—
Coupled with fantasies
Expressed with certainties of the body and the soul.
Can only be remembered—
in a woman alone

Remember? The woman remembers how she gave her love—
with silent expectations
How she dreamed a mother's dream—
of infants spilling milk on the washed floors
of the corner home and the visits to the store—
With clawing urchins-clutching at the windmills of her dress
The man—remembers dreams cast in a
fine mold with emotions shared in body motions
Yet the warmth of remembrances and shattered dreams—
Drift among his memories.

Santa Rosa, 1973

These Streets

I walk

The memory
Raining in my ear

Splattering against my footsteps

In these same streets

Did my feet, splattering rain, make the same noise . . . then?

So, my joys, now shadow greys of
drooping flowers sinking to the depths . . . of my stomach

I walk these same streets

This time

Only with my . . .

Profiling to an empty image

Of my pots, cold, standing listless on the stove

Next to my shadow

Paris, 2008

Life and the Deep Blue

The air, profound,
pine droplets caress my brow—
the wind ruffles the ends of my hair—

My head tilts toward the sky—
such a deep blue that tears
respond to the freedom and
eternal rays of life fill my body!

Something gently suggests that life
means more than the
machines that control us.

San Francisco, 1990

Conformed Chirping

Looking out the window of a new morning—
the vividly clear morning enlightened by a chorus of
birds singing somewhere overhead—

Somehow the voices of birds instruct me to
listen to my true self—

Not who I'm supposed to be or what I'm
                supposed to possess
in order to be a full-fledged member of the group,

group pressure to conform into little atomic robots
                is sometimes unbearable—
                is often unbearable—

and not liveable—

San Francisco, 1983

Pretending Shadow

Shadow of myself—
peaceful, or pretending to be
thinking or pretending to be
caring or pretending to care
loving or pretending to love
Shadow of myself.

San Francisco, 1988

Magic Potion

I lost myself in the maze again
The absurdity of it all,
as though I would cry,
Instead a belly laugh explodes
to cover my hidden fears,
fears—frustrations disappointments—
disappointed because we didn't go until the very end
until the end of the dream.

I lost myself in the maze again
And now we are forced to accept a lesser being
that which we are not
Rusty door knobs—turning into the grating
Endless withering like steel laughter,
Wounded victim unfurling dynasty—
patience gone—wasted finding it somewhere—
reaching into the pillowy silk-lined box of the cloud—
while the truth lay there smiling—smiling.

Paris, 1977

A Single Moment Stops

Time is the ultimate exponent in a wave
of events which will retrogress at some point in the
future, we are traveling through
space in a circular pattern, and after each pass of
the circle we are re-born and the outline of
the circle takes on a darker hue.

I arrived at this as I strolled
through a neighborhood in Santa Rosa, where I once
played. I caught myself walking in the same
footsteps and seeing the world through the same
eyes as I had nine years earlier. The street lamps
still stared at me and the ancient houses reeked,
with ruddy frames with faded white exteriors,
surrounded by scraggly bushes, floored by unkempt
lawns, shrouded with dandelions, weaving a soft
carpet over the bright green stalks. And the leaves
smothered the tiny cement walkways leading up
to the old but stalwart porches.

Even the air smelled the same, the crisp leaves burning
filled my nose as the frosty air screamed with Christmas,
and all those amnesiac delights of a winter wonderland
eating chestnuts while watching "A Christmas Carol",
making pine wreaths for our doors, tracking in mud
on the solid green rug.

tears blurred, recollected all the
frenzies of my impetuous youth. I envisioned myself
clenching the football tightly to my chest as I
maneuvered around my opponents. Before I reached
the broken-down Buick, which marked the goal-line,
the football was replaced by a large
shopping bag, the intense expression on my
face replaced by a pirate's mask. Then the shopping
bag became an egg carton my urchin
face splashed with anxiety's shyness.

I was casually swept into serene depths of the past.
By the wish of a benign spirit, I became a child—
gliding over hedges, carelessly flapping at a low-flying butterfly,
hiding from approaching cars, quickly scurrying
across the street to heaven in the dark; timelessness,
creeping into my ageless body, like the cold morning
dew impregnating the moist slug, creeping-creeping
dragging in no direction, just churning the fine
fibers of its skin, leaving a long trail, which dries and
leaves a crusty path.

Santa Rosa, 1971

Motel

Intrigued by the sound of your smile
I opened the door with our flesh wounds soared
And against my will the heat of your desire
I turned and betrayed the calm in your—in my eyes,
reflecting meadowy streams.
The country seems the better of us—all alone
but never leaving the little juniper die—
beneath the oak—the earth—rock damp
richness of the odious melody of nature
gleaming in my eyes—rocking me to sleep with pollen
sexual palpitations smells—of raw seeping pollen
carried from flower to flower,
into your protective arms,
soothing my dream for eternity and peace
And then—whom do I see but lady desire
to tie me into a knot and fire
me with precious tombstones of life in a corner—
No, ma petite—my dreams unfulfilled
too many cars in the parking lot—
I guess I'll melt down the trickling spring
until I hit bottom of a new world.

Santa Rosa, 1975

Lonely Rage

Awakened by the turn
of your body
against the wooden sides of the
aged bed
the smell of sleep
reposing eye shadows of the past
I wonder if I can change everything
so we could finally be at peace.
What is this rage to live
to the rhythm of a new game?
Game, games, games
an hour at the bar beating our brows.

Lord when the moon
and the nightingale shares its song
a boy in the ghetto streets
a new victim
of the rage to live
is bathed in secrets of love.

Love forgotten, forgetting,
forgetting me, aged grandmother
I haven't forgotten how my parents
just blinked when the pound took
my dog away.

I'm crying to be calmed by
the hand of a love
that is blind and deaf
Trapped by who knows what,
I say to you, Dad,
I am alone.

Santa Rosa, 1974

Black Sicilian

Your black mane-
gently waives before me
your smile
sincere
sweeps the
mournful clouds from my eyes

forgive me-
for you are the dearest of them all-
for your love
    I die slowly-
    painfully-

as I write these words
speckled with tears
with hopes so high

that I cannot live
before the torment
and surprise
in your eyes
upon seeing me that night

and then,
the morning gloom,
the reality of our end
in the shadows ...

Paris 2004

Country Wine

Curious blend of fever—undulations—
Calm,-storm clouds-calm—
Ivory milky full-replenished clouds—
Hovering above me as I build the fence—
My partner sweating—wiping drops away with the back of his hand
Squinting into the sun—
Sipping on a cool beer—
A breeze coming up-saves us another day-
Bending our bodies to the tune of electric handsaws—
Grating and sawdust veiling the air
Thoughts of relaxing after a hard day—
Before the T.V. or
Maybe at the old watering hole
At the corner of Winter Lane and Cherry Tree Boulevard—
Or just sitting on the sofa
With my lady
Her warm brown eyes intently watching mine-
In the silence
While a myriad of revolutions aglow
In country wine.

Santa Rosa, 1972

Nude Before the World

Let thy life seek its course-
though within the eye of the hurricane-
the calm is forever present.
Ah yes the calm-I cry out my insides quiver-

I am outside the body, clothes which protect
my body with hiding, shadowing efficiency-
no longer sheltered-the roof leaks
and joy-the realities-the wet cold, warm
rays of mothers' touch now embracing my
tired frame-

Paris, 1978

Time Had No Meaning

After all those years
our passions to taste
    the surge of life
           ripe and gushing, tempting
           sumptuously
           enticing me
           with your craziness
           passion without form
           without reason
                precluded the necessity
                of time

           time had no meaning.

San Francisco, 1986

Ma Fille

L'arbre silencieux
Like a shadow
Love,

     You lobby for love

To bring us hence
     into one

Your mother and I

But, programmed passion?

How can it be?

Once radiant . . . embrace

Turned cold

Like the ashes

of

Yesterday's campfire . . .

Not your fault

Ma fille
Ma fille

No more hope

But you

And me.

Paris, 2008

Shorties

The Dancer

The girl was entranced by the music,
    dancing wildly across the room,
        her hips revolving around and around
        her eyes fixed on an unknown object in space
            glistening with content and happiness.

White Froth

The illuminated waves pounding the distant shore,
    reveled in the moonlight,
    slamming their cold hands against the
    sea-torn rocks
        their tops indented with tiny crevices,
            inhabited by glistening tide pools.

Santa Rosa, 1968

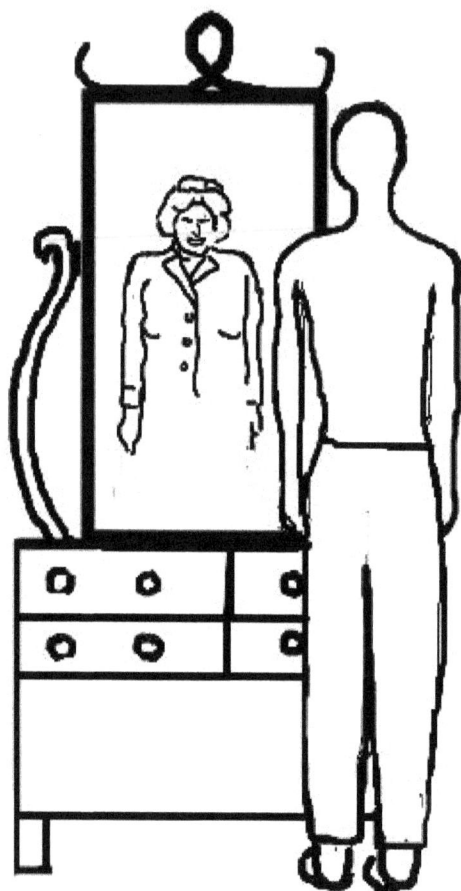

To Auntie,

After all the roads followed
Winding into dead-ends, coolly poised
For another surge into the unknown
Smell of violets gently beneath the entrance
At Maison-laFittes
Before the "Fete" I announced
I am lost, Auntie
Be honest!
I am lost, baby.
I must find it—what? I don't know.

Auntie, I suffered in Morocco
And I turned in green lights—bathed in
Tea and sugar cookies—
And they tried to crucify me—
And I learned from my impurities.
So vast that a candle couldn't light the path.
That the magician sounded in dogmatic rhythms
Heal—heal—heal
My way!

And that (they told me) my Father and Mother lied—
And my name wasn't Frank
That the sky is black and so the
Reflection of my being—

Oh, Auntie—I slowly withered the
Silent softness in the plains of "Maghreb"
Where the sun sets in a bowl of cream-colored strawberries—
And they fed me hypnotic lotions of
anguish and self-flogging virtues—
screened by God who caressed the last
part of me—that remained pure
my love for truth-in-God shedding a tear on
dogmatic intolerance—
and giving strength to beseech his grace

and behold the meditations that shook my withered frame
my hunger for truth
grasped me up 'til the sky—
and shattered my misery with the
caress of infinite wisdom—
the integration of the first and the last
of good and bad
and my bowels wept—torn, strained and my intestines
pained as the acid withdrew
and the light cast a shadow
as the bird in the cage—I was protected
forever by the faith
from the predator
tearing away his grip from my throat—
from my heart.

Love,

Frankie

Paris, 1980

Whim?

Were you just a whim
to be traded
for a sunny day?

or more
than a whim,
more than the earth

from the shores
of the Mediterranean
to the Italian district
in San Francisco

We fought for
    a reason
           to love

infinitely ambiguous
clarified without clarity
    like a cloud
    hugging the earth
         one obscure day

San Francisco, 1988

My Squaw

My squaw in the rugged turf,
you, making a dam of a cool spring on the side of the hill,
creating something, playing in the mud,
sloshing, patting, your hands skillfully managing
your work, as they stroked my body,
rubbing the spring water into my veins melted in thin layers,
easing the tension of a million decibels,
And to tell me I left you there, on the side of the mountain,

Enveloping you and sounding earth waves,
drying my dampened eyes before leaving you, escaping across the
                                                                                    ocean
to conquer Europe, thrashing my last hopes to the ground,
grinding my body into a thin layer of hope,
immersing myself in the richness of your olive oil caress,
caress, embrace, and me crying like a baby,
with desire, mother's womb, flesh, earth tones in me,
silently standing by me,
and then goodbye

As creatures earth digs a present love,
in the future pond of infinite conquest,
me, a man of infant's visions,
I desperately seek the dam, caved in now,
No spring in sight along this dry, lonely hill
Only touch of life is a lone blade of grass, tenderly
Silently bent away from a breeze wafting through the grooved
                                                                                    earth,
my Squaw, my Squaw, my Squaw…....

San Francisco, 1983

129

In the Wind

Cool, refreshing

Star wave brushed my face.

whispering into my ear—

the wind,

something sweet

something simple

If all else fails—

the wind cares

San Francisco, 1983

Silenced

when
the
creative juices
refuse
to
flow
quagmired
befuddled
succumbing
to the
stagnant
pond
of clichés
mental laziness
of
muddy metaphors
safe; but
placid
fecal
programming
machines
cesspools
machines
cesspools
software
cesspools
mechanical games
playing themselves
    to death
wizened and silent.

San Francisco, 1988

La Chambre Blue

Six thousand miles away
I feel your earth waves—
entreating me to step into
your world
another world
a feverish "gamme" of boutiques
symphony halls, opera houses,
elite, Left Bank circles
of writers, painters and the like—
Yet I long for the other side of you
that which awakened me
the beauty of your simplicity
and
searching for beauty
in the corner of
the chamber blue
a little place
tucked far away in the sky
perched over the river Seine.

Ashland, 1981

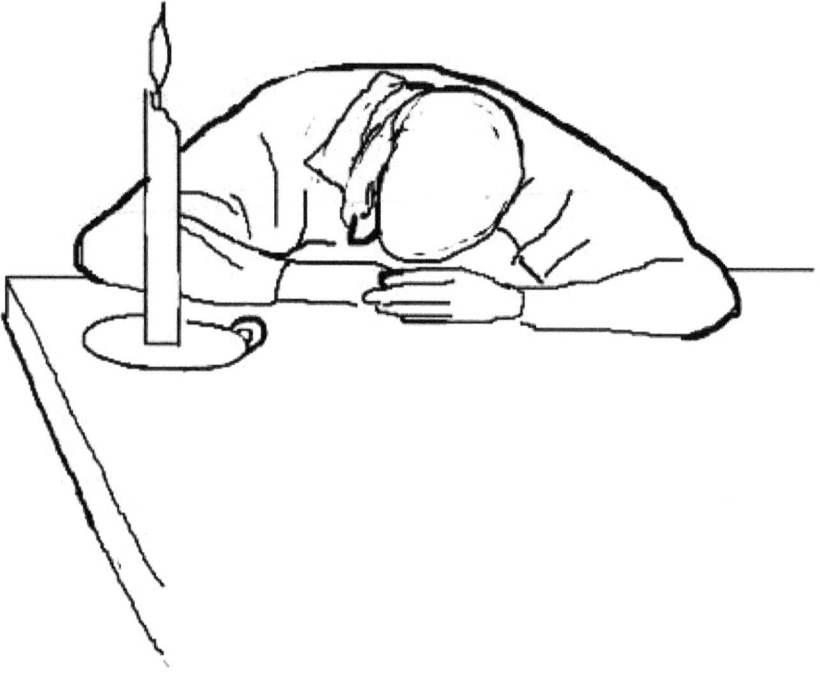

Behind the Silk Curtain

Here I am for the 100th time
on the Champs Elysee.
It is the night before Christmas
and I'm sober as hell.
The dreary lights parade on all sides of the streets
spotted with "the tourist set".

I am a Parisian—I live here.

I ignore a McDonald's stand.
What nerve—planting a
crud-burger in the middle of things.
I walk away from the "Arche de Triomphe"
where an American family flashes clashes chocolate-stained—
"Daddy, looky-looky-I want an ice cream.
Wow-hey-let's go to the Latin Quarter."
The horde runs in circles around Mommy and Daddy,
playing hopscotch—turning in circles
singin' twistin' pointing hopping—

To avoid them, I turn down a side road
bypassing the Concorde
where thousands had been beheaded in 1789.
Across the Seine and through the small streets in the 7th district
seeing small well-kept boutiques, art galleries,
well-designed antiques rococo furniture
through streets smelling of an ancient bourgeois society
small cafes' elite nooks
where artists and philosophers
still come to display their intellectual hardware.

135

Down "rue du Bac" I hear a group of Parisians speaking
in low voices—that juicy French chirping.
I arrive home, close the door
turn on the desk lamp
A shadow slowly bows as
tears form a glistening puddle
among the papers and books—
the street lamp peers through the silk curtains
running a chill through my quivering side.

Paris, 1977

Cronkite Beach

Gone—
Ocean's arms- spraying rose on pale cheeks

Warm kisses contrast the crashing waves

Distant booming

    It can't be so
    It's all gone

Don't ever leave

    Can't forget

Burns inside

At remembering

Each time

    I can't forget

If I do

Then I'm numb

Until death

Frees me

    to feel

again

Paris, 2008

About the Author

FRANK ROMANO earned a PhD at University of Paris I, Panthéon Sorbonne, and a JD at Golden Gate University, Faculty of Law, San Francisco. He is a retired Maître de conférences (assistant tenured professor) at the Université Paris Nanterre in the Anglo-American Literature and Civilization Department, an adjunct professor at Golden Gate University, Faculty of Law and a member of the California and Marseille Bars. He taught literature, history, law and philosophy of law at the Université Paris Nanterre and practices law in France and in the United States. The author actively organizes and participates in interfaith events involving Jews, Moslems, Christians and people of other faiths in Israel and Palestine. He recently attempted to prevent an Israel government bulldozer from destroying "Al khan al Ahmar," a Bedouin village in the West Bank. He was imprisoned, prosecuted and eventually deported to France. Dr. Romano has also authored a book entitled *Storm Over Morocco*, published by AB Film Publishing, *Dans l'ombre du muezzin* [In the Shadow of the Muezzin (published in French by L'Harmattan in April, 2014)], *Globalization of Antitrust Policies* (Mondialisation des politiques de concurrence), published by L'Harmattan in French and a book of poems entitled *Crossing Over* published by World Audience, Inc. He has written many articles published in Europe and in the United States where he is often invited to speak at conferences. He can be reached at: frankfro@aol.com.

www.ingramcontent.com/pod-product-compliance
Lightning Source LLC
Chambersburg PA
CBHW071546040426
42452CB00008B/1098